Papiers
à la
Mode

Papiers à la Mode

Isabelle de Borchgrave & Rita Brown

Bellew Publishing London

This edition published by Bellew Publishing Company Ltd.
8 Balham Hill, London SW12 9EA.

First published by Isabelle de Borchgrave sprl
52 rue Gachard, 1050 Brussels.

Copyright © 2000 Isabelle de Borchgrave, Rita Brown and
Andreas von Einsiedel.

Exhibitions:
Musée de l'Impression sur Etoffes, Mulhouse, France
Museum of Fine Arts, Boston
The Fashion Institute of Technology, New York
Hôtel Braquenié, Paris
The Victoria and Albert Museum, London

ISBN 1 85725 1520

Cover and additional design by Valentina Ruggiero
Printed in Spain by Graficas Syl

The Dresses shown in this catalogue were inspired by original
pieces in the collection of the Fashion Institute of Technology
in New York (p. 44 - 45); the Hermitage, St. Petersburg, Russia
(p.31); Martin Kramer, Switzerland (p.14-15); the Kyoto
Costume Institute, Japan (p.16-17, 22-23, 28-29, 34, 48); the
Metropolitan Museum of Fine Art, New York (p.20-21, 40-41,
49, 50-51), Musée de l'Impression sur Etoffes, Mulhouse
(p. 36-37), the Snowshill Manor collection, National Trust,
England (p.35) and the Victoria and Albert Museum, London
(p.11, 12-13, 52-53). Waistcoats and accessories are creative
interpretations by Isabelle de Borchgrave. The Mulhouse dress
(p. 36-37) is an interpretation by Rita Brown, and the dresses
on p. 54-55 are original designs by Isabelle de Borchgrave.

Our special thanks go to Christine and Mickey Boël,
Laurie Chester, Lisa Fingeret, Douglas Stevens and Ruedi
Wolfensberger for their enthusiastic and friendly support.

Papiers à la Mode

Papiers à la Mode is a fashion parade full of delights - an ephemeral, never-to-be-worn celebration of dresses from the 17th to the 20th century. They are not made of the customary fabrics of high fashion but entirely of paper. The Victoria and Albert Museum's notable collection of fashionable dress together with other leading collections in America, France and Japan inspired Isabelle de Borchgrave and Rita Brown to compose their very own fashion history of life-size dresses in paper in which their devotion to fashion is immediately apparent and contagious. The artists' boundless enthusiasm for their subject is based upon a professional understanding of the decorative appeal of clothes and textiles and expertise in the cutting and construction of garments.

These paper fantasies are perfect illustrations of how the past can inform the present and how works from museums can be re-interpreted in a magical way. The respective skills and imagination of artist-designer Isabelle and the theatrical costumier and conservator Rita enables them to capture the spirit of a dress, its time and its designer. Yet each paper gown has an independent identity being a sumptuous three dimensional artwork born of their special vision.

Valerie D. Mendes

L'atelier

The creative process and making-up resemble activities in a fashion designer's atelier without the anxieties of searching for a multitude of fabrics and trimmings. After initial sketches and trial paper swatches, plain white lengths of dressmaker's drafting paper are transformed by Isabelle with brush, paint and verve into vibrant 'yardage'. Many ingenious techniques are employed to achieve the essence of smudgy warp-printed silks, bold deckchair stripes, delicate floral prints and ethereal laces. A variety of lightweight papers are employed to suggest organza collars, lace engageantes or embroidered voile oversleeves. Texture is attained by crimping, pleating, crumpling and careful scissor work. Rita, with her knowledge and her experience of historical dress, takes the final steps cutting out each delicate garment and assembling it, not with needle and thread, but glue. Out of their escapist wardrobe step a luscious, mid-18th century red and gold Venetian court dress, a summery pink and white evening dress of about 1829-31 and a crispy tailored, sea-side costume of around 1900. This is a fashion show of the imagination which enriches our perception of the history of dress and its importance for design today.

Valerie D. Mendes

The Exhibitions

Brussels is the capital of Europe, but of late it has also been a hotbed of a global artistic collaboration. Belgium, Canada, Japan, Switzerland, the United States of America, England and France have been involved.

Papiers à la Mode - une petite histoire de la mode? No! Not at all. This exhibition is not a didactic exercise. It is fantasy and joy. It is the fruit of the imagination of a talented artist with a great love and passion for fabric and fashion.

About five years ago Isabelle de Borchgrave came across an exhibition catalogue with the title Revolution in Fashion published by the Kyoto Costume Institute. It was fatal, Isabelle fell in love, got inspired and besotted. She decided to recreate some of the sumptuous dresses shown on the pages of this catalogue. The collections and catalogues of the Costume Institute of the Metropolitan Museum and the Fashion Institute of Technology, both of New York, as well as the Victoria and Albert Museum in London, provided added inspiration and models, as did the Musée de l'Impression sur Etoffes, in Mulhouse.

Being a passionate painter she decided to use paper and paint instead of silks and satins. Isabelle went to work and started to experiment and with great verve put brush to paper. Her innate sense of beauty, colour, line and proportion led the way. Over the past few years, in an ongoing project, with the help of Rita Brown - a Canadian theatre costumier - she started turning white sheets of drafting paper into three-dimensional paper sculptures. Clothes are wrapping for the body. And as Isabelle has often designed wrapping papers, this endeavour can be seen as a logical step in her artistic quest.

The resulting dresses are true to their inspirations. The shapes and silhouettes are a perfect interpretation of their historic models.

Simple paper and paint, mixed with imagination and style with added dashes of wit and humour and: voilà you have Papiers à la Mode, an exhibition and book for you to enjoy.

Martin Kamer

1620

Brocart de soie italienne

Venetian court dress, c. 1745

1745

Moire de soie rouge
avec des broderies baroque
venitienne
provenant en dentelle de Milan
Panier à la Watteau
collection Nouvier — maintenant martin Kamer

15

1765
Chiné soie à la française
Lyon silk Chiné
Engageante Alençon lace
Kyoto

Man's waistcoat, c. 1765

Robe à l'anglaise, c. 1770

Robe à la française, c. 1780

Robe à l'anglaise
Interprétation d'un Arbre de Vie,
Braquenié, c. 1760

Pierrot jacket and white cotton petticoat, c. 1790

French round gown, c. 1795

Broderie Anglaise dress and Russian shawl, c. 1812

Taffetas écossais, c. 1810

Robe du soir brodée d'or, c. 1810

English evening dress of the 1850's

1840's dress
Interprétation d'un échantillon de tissu imprimé à Mulhouse

Cafetan, c. 1860
Interprétation du tissu Alcazar, coll. Pierre Frey, Paris

French evening dress by Worth from 1898

Beige linen suit, c. 1900, in an American Navy style

PAUL POIRET

a Paris

Collection Metropolitan Museum

Poiret 1912
Satin lamp shade Dress
Silk Satin & Beaded Flowers
embroider

French silk satin evening dress by Callot Soeurs, Paris, c. 1908

Evening dress by Callot Soeurs, early 1920's

FRONT BODICE 1921
PURPLE + SILVER

1921
Liberty
Mauve silk woven
with gold + silver

1921 SKIRT BACK

Bodice Back 1921
Purple & Silver

Jacket and dress, Fortuny Delphos, 1930's

Création Isabelle de Borchgrave, 1998

Septembre 1999
Robe de Mariée
en papier
Printemps 2000
Trompe l'œil
de guipure
de Satin de soie
de dentelle
iridescente

Le dos est une
surprise
à découvrir
à l'hôtel Braquenié
a partir
du 22 Octobre 99
à l'occasion
de l'exposition
"Papier à la Mode"

Isabelle de Borchgrave

Pour l'an 2000
Robe de mariée, Création Isabelle de Borchgrave

Isabelle de Borchgrave, a Belgian painter and designer, established her studio in Brussels where she studied at the Academy of Fine Arts in the 1970's. Her career includes regular exhibitions of her paintings, costume designs for the Ballet and Theatre, as well as numerous residential and commercial designs throughout Europe. Since 1983, her unique creations of hand-painted fabrics have evolved into the production of furnishing fabrics and designs for the home. Isabelle's current work focuses on the 'Isabelle de Borchgrave' home collection.

Canadian Rita Brown studied costume design history and design in London. For thirty years she has worked as a theatrical costumier mainly with the Shaw Festival Theatre in Ontario where she was also Head of Wardrobe. She has been an advisor and guest lecturer at various theatre schools and in 1990 was the recipient of a Canada Council grant. In recent years she has specialised in costume and textile restoration in London and New York.